SO-BJQ-926

Bilbao

EX·LIBRIS

THE·MEMORIAL·ART·GALLERY

THE UNIVERSITY
OF ROCHESTER

Editorial Everest would like to thank you for purchasing this book. It has been created by an extensive and complete publishing team made up of photographers, illustrators and authors specialised in the field of tourism, together with our modern cartography department. Everest guarantees that the contents of this work were completely up to date at the time of going to press, and we would like to invite you to send us any information that helps us to improve our publications, so that we may always offer QUALITY TOURISM.

QUALITY
TOURISM
WITH
EVEREST

Please send your comments to:
Editorial Everest. Dpto. de Turismo
Apartado 339 – 24080 León (Spain)
Or e-mail them to us at turismo@everest.es

"An Englishman came to Bilbao to see the ria and sea
but when he saw the Bilbao lasses he was loath to leave…
A Bilbao lass, with her pretty face, grace and wit
is worth more than all the American girls with their riches and gold…"

(A popular song, "bilbainada")

Editorial Management: Raquel López Varela

Editorial coordination: Eva María Fernández Álvarez

Text: Julia Gómez Prieto

Photographs: Gonzalo M. Azumendi, Santiago Yaniz Aramendia
Iñaki Aguirre y Archivo Everest

Diagrams: José Manuel Núñez

Cover design: Francisco A. Morais

Cartography: © Everest

Translated by: Babyl Traducciones

All rights reserved. No part of this book may be reproduced, stored
in a retrieval system, or transmitted, in any form or by any means,
electronic, mechanical, photocopying, recording or otherwise,
without the prior written permission of the holders of the Copyright.
This book is sold subject to the condition that it shall not, by way of trade or
otherwise, be lent, re-sold, hired out, or otherwise circulate without the
publisher's prior consent.

© EDITORIAL EVEREST, S. A.
Carretera León-La Coruña, km 5 - LEÓN
ISBN: 84-241-0342-4
Depósito legal: LE. 344 - 2003
Printed in Spain

EDITORIAL EVERGRÁFICAS, S. L.
Carretera León-La Coruña, km 5
LEÓN (Spain)

Key (from the engraving):

...tiago.	5. S: Nicolas.
Ant: Abad	6. S: Iuan d Viejo.
...rancisco.	7. S: Augustin.
...Iuan	8. S: Bizente.
	9. N S: de Begoña.
	10. La Esperanza.
	11. La Cruz.
	12. La Encarnacion.

VISTA.
DE LA MVY NOBLE VILLA
DE.
BILBAO

13. La Concepcion.	17. La Renteria.
14. La Merced.	18. La Casa Consist...
15. S: Monica.	19. El Hospital.
16. L: Plaza.	20. El Arenal.
21. Bilbao la V...	
22. El Puente...	
23. Caminos...	
24. Archand...	

Classical view of Bilbao in the XVIII century, according to a drawing by Thomas Morony of 1784.

THE FOUNDING OF THE CITY AND ITS EXPANSION

The territory now occupied by the **City of Bilbao** has been populated since ancient times, long before its founding as a township. Such is the conclusion that may be drawn from the scarce but telling archaeological finds made in its subsoil.

The history of Bilbao properly speaking, however, dates from the dawning of the Middle Ages, when it began to develop as a trading centre. Its initial development may also have been influenced by the Pilgrims' Route leading along the coast to Santiago de Compostela, the coming and going of the faithful giving rise to intense commercial and cultural activity. Bilbao was also undoubtedly shaped by the Castilian yearning for an outlet to the sea, and acted as a port of entry for foreign merchandise on its way to the Fairs of Castile and a port of departure for Castilian wool exports to the countries of central and northern Europe.

At that time a seafaring village, Bilbao was granted the status of township by Privilege of Diego López de Haro V, Lord of Biscay, dated in Valladolid on 15th June 1300, whereby it was conceded the Fuero de Logroño in what was its own *Founding Charter*.

The Charter conceded the new township complete jurisdiction over the ria of the Nervion, which therefore became known as the *Ria of Bilbao.* Its municipal limits took in the lower Nervion valley, i. e., what is today *Greater Bilbao,* a geographical reality clearly envisaged by the founder of the original township.

The birth and development of Bilbao is closely linked to lie of its land. The city's growth has had to adapt itself to the surrounding ria and mountains at all times.

The river Nervion arises on the Castilian meseta, and then hurls itself over spectacular waterfalls in the Alava valley of **Délica,** close to Orduña. It is converted into a ria or estuary by the influence of the tides and receives salt water about 14 kms before flowing into the sea. It is exactly at this point where Bilbao was initially established, snugly protected from invaders and pirates. And it is precisely the tides that still allow vessels to ply the waters upriver at high tide in search of a safe refuge and trading port. Thus was Bilbao born and it then spread along the river, never straying far from the iron mines and ironworks that were its main trading wealth. The city was therefore born thanks to its sound strategic position and navigable ria, which allowed it to offer Biscayan and Castilian trade a safe outlet to the sea and a privileged link to international trading routes.

In the C15th and C16th Bilbao became the dynamic centre of the whole Seigneury; its ships, ironworks, shipyards and merchandise turned it into a bustling city that received official recognition in 1511 when Queen Juana granted it its own *Consulado de Comercio* (Mercantile Court) and *Casa de Contratación* (House of Trade).

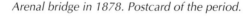

Arenal bridge in 1878. Postcard of the period.

San Antón church and its bridge in the XIX century. Engraving of J.E. Delmas.

The city's merchants set up a businessmen's guild and kept up thriving relations with Bruges, Nantes and other coastal cities of Atlantic Europe. Then came trade with England and later with the South American colonies. Bilbao and its Seigneury thereby became involved in the *Carrera de las Indias,* the trade convoy to the New World.

As trade increased and the ships grew bigger, the marine trading points spread away from the inner wharves of the ria as far as the old bridge of San Antón. Little by little the port of Bilbao handed over its functions to other areas of the ria closer to the sea, until the main trading centres were eventually set up in today's *Superport of Santurtzi.*

From the wharves of the **Casco Viejo** or Old City, Bilbao kept up its trading relations with northern Europe during the late Middle Ages and its Atlantic trade in the first centuries of the Modern era. This trade and navigation gave rise not only to merchants but also to ship owners and first rate pilots; masters and captains of great international prestige who plied the waters along all compass bearings from the Baltic to the West Indies and from Iceland to the Indian Ocean.

The populous district of **Atxuri,** on the right-hand bank of the ria and close to the Church of San Antón has always been the city's most important entrance point . It was in this part of the city where the French and Castilian routes converged, and it was from here that pilgrims on their way to Santiago, traders and travellers alike, would set off on their journeys.

The **Escuela de Artes y Oficios** (Arts and Crafts School), which used to give refuge to the pilgrims heading for Santiago, was the *City's Santo Hospital Civil* from 1480 onwards, and subsequently was rebuilt in 1818 with a stern Neoclassical layout of ashlar stones. It was a museum and then a teaching centre. Built into a side wall close to the stairway is a Neoclassical fountain designed by Paret y Alcazar, a renowned painter who lived and worked in Bilbao in the C18th during the reign of Carlos III. Some of his pictures may be seen in the **Museo de Bellas Artes** (Fine Arts Museum).

Two original and excellent civil buildings grace the district of Atxuri. The first is the **Escuelas del Maestro García Rivero,** built by the architect Pedro de Ispizua at the start of the century in an eclectic style with interesting sculptural adornments. The second, from the same epoch, is the **Estación de los Ferrocariles Vascos** (Basque Railway Station) on the Bilbao-San Sebastián line, built by Leonardo Rucabado in Basque regional style.

The **Church of La Encarnación,** in the square of the same name, forms part of the old Dominican Monastery, today converted into the **Museo Sacro** (Holy Museum). The church is a good example of the Basque Gothic style of the C16th. The doorway, in Renaissance style with a certain Baroque air, is framed in an enormous arch that recalls other Bilbao churches, such as **San Vicente** or the **Basilica de Begoña.** The main front is topped off by a bell-tower-like steeple. The spacious, elegant interior has a nave and two aisles and a ribbed vault supported on great, cylindrical columns. The **Museo Diocesano de Arte Sacro** was opened in 1995 and is housed in the old Dominican Monastery, next to the church, whose construction dates back to the C16th. It contains the ecclesiastical artistic treasures of the diocese, deliberately brought here to prevent their deterioration. The museum is built around the monastery's old cloister, with two wings especially fitted out for the purpose. The first floor has excellent exhibits of silver liturgical objects taken from 51 churches of the diocese, plus a rich, varied collection of religious ornaments and costumes from the C16th to C20th.

The second floor is dedicated to religious art down the ages: images, painting, sculpture, architecture. Especially attractive is the small room exhibiting the *Andra Maris* or medieval carvings depicting the Virgin Mary, with a selection from the C13th to C16th. There is also an interesting exhibit of sculptures in the Hispanic-Flemish and Renaissance style. A special mention must go to the C18th century picture collection, with religious motifs attributed to Lucas Jordan.

▼ *View of the old quarters.* *The Naja piers in front of the old quarters.* ▶

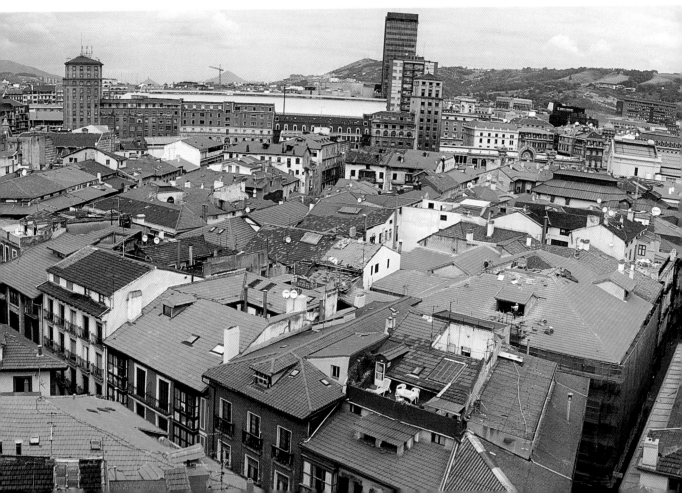

DISCOVERING THE CASCO VIEJO (OLD CITY)

Originally located on the left-hand bank, now known as Bilbao la Vieja or Old Bilbao, the centre of city then shifted to the Nervion's right-hand bank, already a ria, into land belonging to the old municipal district of Begoña. The initial walled town developed close to the bridge and alcázar (fortified building) where the **Church of San Antón** stands today. A tower marked the end of each of the original streets of that township: **Somera** or upper street, **Artecalle** or middle street and **Tendería,** the most commercial of the three. The bend of the river was thus a natural defensive moat and its banks afforded a site for the mooring, loading and unloading of ships.

Allendesalazar Palace.

Steps that allow communication between the mountain and the narrow tidal inlet.

One of the many commercial streets of the old quarters of Bilbao.

These first three streets were crossed by cantones (cross streets) that formed a simple but complete urban layout with regular building plots. The original church of this township was that of **Santiago,** where the cathedral of the same name stands today.

The surrounding walls served not only for defence but also for territorial demarcation. The **Calle de la Ronda** took its name and form from the outer walled circuit. On this street stands the house where Miguel de Unamuno was born, and there is a simple commemorative plaque in honour of this distinguished thinker and writer, born on 29th September 1864.

At the first crossroads stands the **Portal de Zamudio,** marking the spot of the old wall gate on the Zamudio road. This marks the true limit of the original settlement. The slightly curved shaped of Calle Somera proves that it originally followed the line of the outer wall, which is no longer standing. This is one of the most populous streets of old Bilbao, with a host of bars and taverns, where the Bilbao tradition of the *txikiteo* is still kept up, veritable evening *pub crawls* to sample glasses of wine in each bar.

Ribera bridge.

The Church of San Antón rises up over the ría. It is without doubt the most authentic of all Bilbao churches, and its stylised image forms part of the city's coat of arms with the old bridge that used to link both banks. Its construction dates back to the C15th and it is a mixture of Gothic and Renaissance styles with a lovely Plateresque door. The church stands on the site of the old alcázar that used to defend the entrance bridge to the township and was knocked down in 1366 with the first extension of the built-up area.

It is small inside with a wide nave supported on outside flying buttresses and two lower aisles with Gothic ribbed vaults supported on six columns. All the altars were removed years ago, so the interior has a very stern air. Only some images of Juan Pascual de Mena are conserved. Outside, the slim, graceful tower stands out, built in Churrigueresque Baroque style, together with the C16th doorway, with excellent Renaissance lines and beautiful sculptures from the studio of Guiot de Beaugrant.

◀ *San Antón church, the most beloved by the people of Bilbao.*

Elegancy characterizes the bourgeois buildings of old Bilbao.

The Market's glazed window with the shield of the city.

*Paintings in the Arches
of Ribera.*

The **Puente de San Antón** is a symbol of the city together with the church of the same name. The first and original bridge united the old seafaring town with the opposite bank (first expansion of the town). Down the ages it has suffered many floods of the river Nervion during the dreaded "aguaduchos" (spates). Today's bridge, dating from 1878, is built entirely from stone with two great flattened arches. The **Mercado de la Ribera,** or riverside market, is a monumental structure built by the architect Pedro de Ispizua in the twenties. It was raised on what used to be the Plaza Vieja and the open dock market. Access is gained by means of two central stairways and the interior is laid out on several levels and in

Market of Ribera, built towards 1920 over the primitive pier of the harbour.

two wings. The stained glass windows are a notable adornment. A visit to this sanctuary of good eating is always an interesting experience, especially the fish stalls on the ground floor.

The **Museo de Reproducciones Artísticas** contains an original, handsome and singular collection of famous classical and ancient sculptures magnificently reproduced in plaster, enabling the visitor to study all the sculptural styles of Assyrian, Egyptian, Greek, Roman and Renaissance art. It started off as a drawing studio for Fine Arts students and had several different sites. Nowadays it is considered to be the most important museum of its type in Spain.

Michelangelo's Moses, in the Museum of Artistical Reproductions.

Door of the Angel, in the Cathedral, through which passed the pilgrims that went to Santiago de Compostela along the coast.

BILBAO ON THE PILGRIMS' ROUTE TO SANTIAGO

Despite the traditional image of the Pilgrims' Route to Santiago as an exclusively inland affair, the truth is that the Muslim invasion of the peninsula meant that in the first centuries of the Middle Ages the safest and most-used route was the one that followed the Cantabrian coast. Many pilgrims put in to a coastal port and then joined one of the routes leading to St James' tomb.

This tradition has left its mark on several places in the province of Bizkaia (Biscay). Many churches and hermitages bear the name of the saint or others related to the pilgrimage, such as San Roque, San Martín or San Severino. It is also frequent to see iconographic representations of the Apostle Saint, not only as a Pilgrim but also as *Santiago Matamoros* (St James the Moor slayer).

Many sites on the Biscay coastal route are imbued with the spirit of St James. Witness the town of **Markina,** where there was a pilgrim's hospital until the C15th, or **Cenarruza / Ziorta,** whose celebrated collegiate church had annexed to it the best pilgrim's hospital and shelter in the whole province. The interior route passed through the town of **Durango,** whose *Cruz de Gurutzaga* includes amongst its reliefs the image of a St James in pilgrim's attire. The route then ran alongside the river Ibaizabal, entering Bilbao in the **Barrio de Atxuri,** where there was a Pilgrims' Hospital. Across the Puente de San Antón, in the middle of Old Bilbao, a window image of St James on horseback, beneath whose feet the route passed, recalls the age-old devotion to the saint.

Cathedral's vault.

Neogothic tower and facade of the cathedral. ▶

To the left, the Gothic cloister of the Cathedral.

Under, mausoleum of the powerful family of Bilbao called Arana-Varona, in the Cathedral.

The Mother Church of **Señor Santiago** already existed when the township was founded in 1300 and the devotion to St James was deeply rooted in the Bilbao people of that time, as a result of the passing of a pilgrimage route that also sought the venerated image of the *Virgen de Begoña*.

The current Gothic cathedral, of unknown authorship, was laid out over the base of the old Romanesque church. The **Cathedral of Santiago** is the most important church in the city and acquired the status of cathedral in 1949 with the creation of the actual diocese. The cathedral building began life as a church in 1379 and was finished in the early C15th, with an obvious French influence. It was consecrated as a Basilica in 1819 at the behest of Cardinal Gardoqui of Bilbao.

The cathedral interior has a handsome Gothic layout with a nave and two lower aisles adorned with chapels. It has a crossing and a narrow ambulatory joined to the main altar by pointed arches, with polygonal chapels of varying sizes. The vaults have ribs and liernes and rest on cylindrical columns with built-in pilasters.

Solemn mass celebrated in the Cathedral with occasion of the reopening of the worship of the temple after its complete restoration in 2000.

The crossing is right in the centre of the general ground plan. In the C18th the church was extended by adding a choir and the chapels behind the main door. It has a galleried triforium with openwork parapet surrounding the whole nave, and it is this feature, together with the ambulatory, that is distinctive of pilgrim churches. The most interesting chapel is that of Pilar, which has the uncorrupted body of San Fructuoso. There is a beautiful C17th pietà by Aboitiz and a moving Christ figure attributed to the Renaissance sculptor Guiot de Beaugrant. There are a number of Gothic burial vaults in other chapels.

The small but beautiful C15th cloister has the purest Gothic style of the whole building, with wide tracery arches and floral decoration on the capitals. The *Puerta del Ángel,* the cloister entrance door from Calle del Correo, is a C16th late Renaissance work with lovely Isabelline lines (i.e. the predominant architecture of the reign of Isabel I "la Católica"). It is the pilgrims' door. The great atrium or portico, characteristic of Basque churches, was built in 1581. This is very wide with giant arcades of semi-circular arches supported on sturdy pilasters that sustain the vaults and serve as an external buttress. They protect a beautiful Gothic door in a side entrance that is not used.

The main front has undergone several modifications. The current one is the work of Severino de Achúcarro in a C19th Neogothic style. The openwork tower, the work of the same architect, blends in well with the rest of the building. The Santa Iglesia Catedral del Señor Santiago, as it is traditionally known, is located right in the middle of the Old Town, its main front overlooking a peaceful square adorned with a monumental C18th Baroque fountain by Luis Paret y Alcázar. Santiago, the apostle St. James, has been the patron saint of Bilbao since 1643, the only city besides Compostela with this patron saint in Spain.

Fountain of the Dog.

THROUGH THE HEART OF CLASSIC BILBAO

The population soon began to outgrow Bilbao's original site. The commercial development that the city experienced in the C15th and C16th forced it to stretch out beyond the confining corset of the walls. In the mid C15th the streets of Belosticalle, Carnicería Vieja, Barrencalle and Barrencalle Barrena evolved parallel to the three original streets. So were born the **Siete Calles,** or Seven Streets, the name commonly given to the Old City.

Subsequent enlargements of the Old City went off in the direction of El Arenal de San Nicolás, so giving rise to the streets of Santa María, Nueva, Torre, etc., and then came the great C18th thoroughfares of Bidebarrieta and its twin Calle del Correo.

Calle de la Torre conserves a notable C17th building, the **Palacio de los Vargas,** popularly known as *La Bolsa*. Nowadays, duly refurbished, it is an exhibition and cultural centre. From its corner you can see the **Basílica de Begoña,** where it used to be a tradition to sing the Hail Mary every evening in honour of the virgin enthroned in the facade.

Calle del Perro, alongside the former, is another symbolic spot of the Old City of Bilbao, famous for its popular Fuente del Perro, a Neoclassical construction dating from 1800, as is recorded in Roman characters on the fountain front. The name of the fountain also served to baptise the street, and refers to the dogs (perros) that adorn its spouts.

Calle Bidebarrieta runs parallel to Calle de Correo. It was laid out to accommodate a C17th expansion of old Bilbao. This small *Gran Vía* or Main Street of the time conserves some of the best mansions of the old city, including the **Palacio de los Mazarredo.** An inscription on its facade, beneath its enormous coat of arms, tells us that here was born Almirante Mazarredo, a distinguished Admiral of the Spanish Navy.

The Correo street shows a splendid bourgeois architecture.

The next block along contains another sumptuous building, the **Municipal Library** and **City Archive,** built in the late C19th as headquarters of the *Sociedad El Sitio.* This "siege society" was set up after the siege suffered by the city during the last Carlist war (January-May 1874), grouping together the voluntary combatants who defended the city. The notable building, Imperial French in style, is the work of the architect Severino de Achucarro and is worth a look inside to see its lobby, staircase, meeting rooms and reading rooms.

Calle del Correo is nowadays the Old City's main pedestrian thoroughfare and shopping centre, uniting Paseo del Arenal with the Cathedral of Santiago. On both sides of the street there are many large and small shops of great tradition. The names of some adjacent streets, Sombrerería, Cinturería (hatmaker, beltmaker) recall the medieval origins and the characteristic trades of the city of Bilbao. They lead in to Plaza Nueva and Calle de la Cruz.

In the C18th new areas of Bilbao began to emerge as important centres of city life. Such is the case of **Plaza Nueva** and **Paseo del Arenal.** The laying out of the latter and **Arrabal de San Nicolás** definitively marked out the limits of the Old City. This whole area was designated a *Historic Artistic Site* in 1972. Apart from its historic significance and its religious architecture, it boasts a splendid collection of civil buildings of great interest.

Local library: assembly hall and glazed window.

*Next double page, terrace atmosphere
in the Nueva Square.*

Partial view of Bilbao with the Arriaga theater in the foreground.

Plaza Nueva is the great arcaded square of Bilbao. It is a noble Neoclassical work with restrained lines. Although designed by Alejo de Miranda in 1784, the various reforms made to the plans meant that it was not finished until 1851. It comprises 64 arches separated by 66 Doric columns supporting three upper floors. One of its sides, that which sports the Biscay Coat of Arms, once housed the Diputación Foral de Bizkaia (Biscay Provincial Government) and today it is the headquarters of the Academia de la Lengua Vasca (Basque Language Academy).

On Sundays it comes alive with stamp markets and other sundry collections, plants and pets. It also stages the Christmas Market and the numerous popular events of the *Aste Nagusia* in August.

These former suburbs of old Bilbao were made up of old fishermen's houses built on a beach in a bend of the river, and were therefore known as the **Arenal** (sandy area) **of San Nicolás.** Once built upon the area became the **Salón del Arenal,** and the boulevard running from **San Nicolás** to the Theatre became the centre of social, financial and cultural life of C19th Bilbao. Today the *Café Boulevard,* in its day the "in" café and renowned gathering place, is reminiscent of those times.

Lime trees and acacias frame the elegant gardens studded with paths and fountains that surround the modernist *bandstand* built by Pedro de Ispizua in 1928, where the Municipal Band stages its Sunday concerts.

*Dome of La Unión and Fénix building
in the Arenal Avenue.*

Above, columns in the Nueva Square.

To the left, peacefulness in the Arenal gardens.

Arenal avenue.

The **Teatro Arriaga** gets its name from the famous Bilbao composer Juan Crisóstomo de Arriaga (1806-1826), called the *Spanish Mozart* due to the precocity of his elegant compositions. The Teatro Arriaga was opened in 1890 on the site of an old theatre called Teatro de la Villa, and is the work of Joaquín Rucoba and Octavio de Toledo. Its eclectic style is inspired by the Opera of Paris, and the interior is richly ornate. With the passing of time the theatre has suffered many disasters, from which it has always managed to bounce back, the last one being a serious flood in 1983. It was then definitively restored to its original

Arriaga theater: Atlases in the side facade.

Details of the back facade.

Arriaga theater. Main facade.

splendour, with the addition of a monumental staircase that has greatly enhanced its artistic value. The Arriaga is currently the Municipal Theatre, a great Cultural Centre with its own stage settings and it puts on an excellent annual programme of top-class concerts, plays, ballets, operas, etc.

The **Church of San Nicolás** and its surroundings make up a characteristic spot of Bilbao and the church itself is one of the best Baroque buildings in Biscay. Built on the land once occupied by an old fishermen's hermitage dedicated to the same saint, another church was raised in about 1490, which suffered various setbacks and floods that jeopardised its very existence. In 1754 the Guipuzcoa architect Ignacio de Ibero y Erquiza won the contract to build a new, more monumental church to replace the former one. The building's original floor plan is octagonal, in line with the Baroque style of the times, albeit with some Renaissance features mixed in. Its doorway is also Baroque although with restrained lines, and is flanked by twin towers with a central belfry, giving a great sense of harmony to the main front with its row of balconies.

Its polygonal interior has a wealth of sculptural work, with magnificent altarpieces carved in walnut and beautiful sculptures. Most of this carving work was entrusted to Pascual de Mena in 1754, making this church a veritable museum of this prestigious sculptor.

In the small **Plaza de San Nicolás** behind the same church a lovely building with a certain French air served as the first head office of **Banco de Bilbao** in 1856. The French architect Lavalle finished it off in

Main facade of San Nicolás, Baroque temple of octagonal floor (XVlll century). ▶

San Nicolás square.

1868 and it was reformed by Severino de Achúcarro between 1881 and 1886. It is an eclectic Classical-cum-Baroque building with great windows and attics. Currently the bank's cultural and exhibition centre, it stands on a corner of the traditional Calle de Ascao, a street that skirts the Plaza de Unamuno and then continues as Calle de la Cruz.

The **Basque Archaeological, Ethnographical and Historical Museum** is to be found in **Calle de la Cruz,** housed in the old building of the *Colegio de San Andrés,* a school which, the forerunner of today's University of Deusto, was run by the Society of Jesus in Bilbao for many years.

The outside of the building is of an almost monastic severity. Inside, the old cloister, restrained and elegant, is formed by a three-tier arcade of semi-circular arches. The dominating feature in the cloister courtyard is the enigmatic, historical idol known as *Mikeldi,* which turned up in excavations near Durango. The cloister arcades exhibit an interesting collection of large noble and municipal coats of arms from old mansions and public buildings. The museum itself is divided into 9 sections taking in the Archaeology, Ethnography and History not only of Biscay but of the whole Basque Country.

The ground floor exhibits a representative sample of stone funeral steles from Biscay burial sites, some dating back to prehistoric times. Another room is given over completely to pastoral culture, deeply rooted in the Basque Country, displaying the uses, customs, the habitat, craftsmanship, beliefs, etc. The first floor's prehistory rooms exhibit finds from excavations in the *caves of Arenaza, Santimamiñe* and *Lumentxa,* which take in the Middle and Upper Palaeolithic, the Bronze Age and Iron Age. Of particular interest is the rich collection of ceramics and pharmacy jars from the factories of Bilbao, Pasajes and Busturia that were working during the C19th, the highlight being a chemist's set of jars and cabinet. Other sections on this floor are the Weapons Room, the Sea Room dedicated to fishing and navigation, the Iron Room with a life-like model of a foundry and a sample of the ironworks production throughout the last centuries.

The most important items on the History of Bilbao are the mementoes of the last Civil War and the Carlist Wars of last century, particularly the sieges the city suffered on both occasions.

The top floor houses the Rooms of the *Consulado de Bilbao* (Mercantile Court and Guild) with the beautiful C18th cabinets where part of the archive of this historical commercial institution is kept, and the great relief model of Biscay, representing with great accuracy the lie of the land and all the towns and villages of Biscay.

The **Church of Los Santos Juanes** is joined onto the History Museum, since it used to be the church of the old San Andrés school. When the Jesuits were expelled from Spain by Carlos III in 1768 it became the parish church of Los Santos Juanes.

Santos Juanes church.

Archaeological, Basque ethnographical and historical museum. Cloister and "Mikeldi", the enigmatic protohistorical idol.

It was built in 1624 to the plans of Martín Ibáñez de Zalbidea in the purest Jesuit style. The austere classical facade has four cylindrical columns supporting a pediment. The interior has a nave with two much lower aisles, and the presbytery is crowned by a handsome pendentive dome decorated with scenes of the life of San Ignacio and other Jesuit saints. The church has a great wealth of Baroque altarpieces. That of the main altar is Churrigueresque with great Solomonic columns and oil paintings attributed to the school of Ribera. The altarpieces of the aisles are C17th and C18th with excellent images and signed paintings. All this was restored after the enormous damage caused by the floods of 1983.

The **Plaza de Miguel de Unamuno** is dedicated to this distinguished thinker and writer from Bilbao, who was born and lived very close by, in Calle de la Ronda. Many pages of his books are dedicated to these corners he loved so much. A simple monument in his honour stands on the spot: the head of Unamuno on an erect column, the work of Victorio Macho. In the centre of the square there is a small classical-style fountain topped by a canopy.

The **Calzadas de Mallona,** whose stairs strike out from the Plaza de Unamuno, leads to the old cemetery of Mallona, of which only a monumental gateway still stands. But the Calzadas ends at the Basílica de la Virgen de Begoña, the female patron saint of Biscay.

The **Basílica de Begoña** stands on the hill of Artagan, on land of the old Republic of Begoña, protecting and dominating old Bilbao.

Rise to Begoña from the Mallona road.

Begoña Basilica, which keeps the patron saint
of Vizcaya, the virgin of Begoña.

Legend has it that the virgin herself appeared in 1519 to point out the spot to raise this votive church over an old hermitage. It was built forthwith in a simple Gothic style, the work of Sancho Martínez de Arego and the master stonemason Juan de Uriona. The church's spacious interior has a nave and two aisles ending in a three-sided apse braced by external buttresses and flying buttresses. The crossing domes are supported on 10 long, slim Gothic columns with capitals.

The main altarpiece is the work of Antonio de Alloytiz and Pedro de la Torre from the last century. It is a splendidly crafted two-piece work with two pairs of fluted columns framing the image of the Virgin of Begoña. The sculpture, of great artistic value, is a typical seated Andra Mari, late C13th Gothic, and 1.17 meters high. With a serene, shining face, great eyes and an incipient smile, the Madonna holds the child Jesus on her lap.

The church door belongs to school of Rodrigo Gil de Hontañón, Plateresque in style, from the end of the C16th. It has a segmental arch between paired columns with a fine effigy of Prudence in the keystone. The main front is topped by a graceful, belfry-like tower made by José M. Basterra in 1907 to replace the one destroyed in the Carlist war of 1874.

Next page, Gothic inside of the Basilica of Begoña.
Solemn mass during the festivity of the Patron Saint.

A STROLL THROUGH MODERN BILBAO

The growth of the city at the end of last century, a phenomenon closely bound up with the opening of the Madrid-Bilbao railway in 1875 and the workforce drawn in by the mining and industrial boom, forced Bilbao to set about the building of its *ensanche* or new suburbs. The first plans date from 1876, drawn up by the architects Severino de Achúcarro, Ernesto Hoffmeyer and Pablo de Alzola. The city was now going to cross the river towards the **Municipal District of Abando** and develop an extensive fluvial terrace on the left-hand bank of the river Nervion.

The old city could not cope with such unexpected growth. Hence the leap across the river to start on the creation of a new, more spacious Bilbao with straight, open streets meeting in circular spaces, avenues, boulevards and tree-lined walks, all built on the fields and orchards of Albia. This is the modern Bilbao, with stately mansions of excellent fin-de-siècle architecture and exemplary town planning…

It became the site of the financial institutions, the stock exchange, the head offices of the shipping, iron and steel, commercial and trading companies…

This elegant expansion zone was to become the visible expression of the architectural talent of the time as each exponent created one fine building after another, whether houses, government offices or commercial premises, sometimes in a mixture of styles that allowed a free eclecticism to hold sway.

Arenal bridge.

Facade of the stock market building.

The first decades of the C20th were propitious for Bilbao, because the economic growth sparked off a parallel cultural movement of unprecedented vigour. Contact with the most important cities of the time, above all London and Paris favoured an artistic blossoming to which the trading and industrial magnates of the time were by no means immune. Poets, painters and sculptors found a rich field for their work and were encouraged to seek new artistic forms. Something of this splendour can still be witnessed in today's city, in its buildings and above all in its museums.

Bilbao after the Spanish Civil War was a city enjoying a spectacular, if somewhat uncontrolled growth, drawing in people from far and wide to fuel an industry in ongoing expansion. The city pushed back its limits, climbed up the nearby mountains, joined up with the neighbouring districts and formed one big conurbation along the river Nervion, from Galdakao to Abra, home today to more than one million people. The greater part of the population of Biscay is packed into this small part of its territory.

The **Puente del Arenal,** skirting the hump of Arenal across the ria, separates the old city from the new. This bridge, with its characteristic lampposts, serves to join both banks and channel the heavy traffic between them. Almost nothing remains of the Puente de Isabel II, which, opened in 1845, represented the first use of iron architecture in Biscay. The Carlist Wars and the last Civil War made several reconstructions necessary.

It is Bilbao's most representative bridge and symbolises the expansion of the old inner city towards the new C20th suburbs. Three emblematic buildings of the new city were raised by the bridge, symbols of three new realities that, in the past, stood for Bilbao's future: the Railway, the Bourgeoisie and Trade.

The construction of the **Santander-Leon Railway Station** coincided with the arrival of the railway, a crucial event for Bilbao and its hinterland. The railway line was constructed to supply the blast furnaces

Glazed window that decorates the Abando Station.

with their essential fuel: coal from the Leon mining fields. The original designs were by the architect Severino de Achúcarro, and the building dates from 1898.

Its style is a subtle blend of classicism and modernism, the former evident in the platform colonnade and the latter in the facade and concourse. The profuse use of coloured glass endows it with a singular beauty.

Opposite the Puente del Arenal, between Calle de Bailén and Calle de Navarra, stands the headquarters of the **Sociedad Bilbaína,** Bilbao's most important private club, an institution of great tradition and prestige, better known in Bilbao as *La Bilbaína*. Historically, it was a club reserved exclusively for the upper middle class, and it has occupied the current site since 1913. It is the work of the architect Emiliano Amann with obvious central European influences.

Its opulent, elegant interior, reserved exclusively for members, has an excellent library and a magnificent collection of local painting.

Part of its ground floor has recently been converted into the Gran Casino Nervión, the only club of its type in Bilbao.

The **Stock Market,** partly joining on to the Sociedad Bilbaína, is housed in a simple but elegant building, where Bilbao's stock exchange does its business, the financial driving force behind the whole city. Bilbao is one of Spain's most important financial centres, and its stock-exchange tradition dates back to last century.

The **Estación de Abando,** also called Estación del Norte, is the most important and most central of all the city's train stations. It is a spartan building, whose facade gives onto the Plaza Circular.

Concordia station, the one of the narrow gauge train.

A great stained-glass window dominates the central access to the platforms, the theme of which is all the facets of Bilbao's economy. The **Plaza Circular,** previously the Plaza de España, marks the point where the city's expansion began. It is presided over by a column-mounted likeness of *Don Diego López de Haro, Señor de Bizkaia,* founder of the city of Bilbao back in 1300; in his hand he holds the *Carta Puebla* or founding charter. It is the work of the sculpture Mariano Benlliure. The square is surrounded by a medley of classical and modern buildings, all belonging to banking and financial institutions, plus the aforementioned Estación Central de Abando. In terms of sheer bulk the building that stands out is the headquarters of the **Banco de Bizkaia,** which, in 1969, replaced a notable 1903 construction by the architect Basterra. A series of thoroughfares leading off from this Plaza Circular defined the development of the so-called *Ensanche,* the new turn-of-the-century Bilbao. The Calle Hurtado de Amézaga leads off towards the higher zones of Torre Urizar and San Adrián, in the direction of the Plaza Zabálburu, and the Calle Buenos Aires leads back to the ria but in the direction of the City Hall.

*Underground entrance ("Fosterito")
in the Circular square.*

Monument to Don Diego López de Haro, founder of the city.

Facades of the Circular square.

The **Gran Vía de Don Diego López de Haro** is the main thoroughfare of Modern Bilbao, the hub of urban life and the heart of the network of streets and squares making up the Ensanche. It is a handsome, tree-lined, well laid-out city street whose buildings on both sides house the most important financial and political institutions and the smartest shops. It is made up of two very different sections, the first, from Plaza Circular to Plaza Elíptica, the oldest part, and the second from the latter square to the Plaza del Sagrado Corazón, which was laid out later.

The zone containing the **Jardines de Albia** was the first square laid out in the new fin-de-siécle Bilbao suburbs. It serves as a reference point for the surrounding network of meticulously designed streets, squares and housing blocks.

Atmosphere at the Iruña café.

Albia is a typical Bilbao corner, the first large square with gardens of modern Bilbao, a leafy, green isle amidst the city traffic. There is a certain Parisian feel about the gardens and houses surrounding it. Dominating the square is a seated statue of Antonio de Trueba, *Antón el de los Cantares,* poet, writer, recorder of regional customs and official chronicler of Biscay during the last century. It is an excellent work by the sculptor Mariano Benlliure.

Close to the Jardines de Albia is the most traditional café of modern Bilbao, the **Café Iruña,** a building with a tradition for discussion circles and cultural life dating back over one hundred years. Of particular interest is its interior decoration in Neo-Caliphal style.

Other notable buildings surround this square, such as the **Palacio de Justicia** (Courthouse), a stern fifties building, once the head office of the **Naviera Sota y Aznar** (shipping company) and now used for institutional purposes. Interesting blocks of flats also surround the square, early C20th buildings with elegant and sometimes monumental facades. **San Vicente Mártir de Abando** was the church of the municipal district of Abando, upon whose land the Bilbao Ensanche was planned. Set in the Jardines de Albia, it is the most traditional church of Modern Bilbao. It was founded in the C12th, but the most ancient surviving part is a Gothic side door of the C14th.

Beautiful facade in the Gran Vía avenue of Bilbao.

The current church is C16th in the so-called Basque-Gothic style. Its harmonious interior has a hall-like nave and aisles, with great Tuscan columns holding up the ribbed vault. The facade is Renaissance in style, with a great central pointed arch framing a rusticated arch doorway topped with pinnacles. The main altar is Neoclassical and has fine sculptures. In one wall of the church Antonio de Trueba is buried.

Alongside the Church of San Vicente stands the **Sabin Etxea** building, which is the headquarters of the Basque Nationalist Party, raised on the same site where, not long ago, the birthplace of Sabino Arana y Goiri stood, founder in 1895 of the nationalist movement in the Basque Country.

The head office of the **Banco de Bilbao** is a sumptuous classical structure with a great Corinthian colonnade running along its whole front; it dominates three streets, including Almeda de Mazarredo. It is perhaps the most impressive private building of the whole Gran Vía of Bilbao. The chamfered corner of the main entrance is crowned by a shrine with a statue of the god Mercury. It is the work of the architect Pedro Guimón and dates from 1922.

Facade of the Bank of Bilbao.

Federico Moyua square or Elliptical square.

The **Palacio de la Diputación Foral** is the headquarters of the most important political institution of Biscay and is also a splendid, opulent building in its own right, along the lines of the eclectic style prevailing at the time of its construction in the early C20th. It is a free-standing building, whose main front is adorned with a great central porch and row of balconies. The whole building is constructed in diamond-cut dressed stone. The interior has an imperial staircase and a wide lobby, decorated with frescoes by Anselmo de Guinea, with stained glass windows and sculptures. The architect was Luis Aladrén.

The **Plaza de (Federico) Moyua** (Plaza Elíptica) is the nerve centre of the modern city, perhaps because it is the hub from which several of the Ensanche's important streets radiate out. Its well-tended classical gardens have always been the most typical feature of the city; even though the construction of the Metro means they have been dug up for 8 years. The Plaza is ringed by some interesting buildings, and from its centre you can see the two most important mountains of Bilbao's outskirts, *Pagasarri,* the highest and, opposite it, the *Monte Artxanda,* a public park and recreation area of the city.

The **Chávarri Palace** is, with no doubt, the most beautiful civil building of Bilbao. It was built towards 1894 as residence of the Chávarri engineer brothers. It was designed by the Dutch architect Paul Hankar and the works were conducted by Atanasio de Anduiza, who developed a great fantasy according to the modernist taste of the period, combining stones and marbles of different tones together with capricious forms of Renaissance style. Nowadays it is the head office of the Civil Government.

The Montero House, work by Luis Aladrén (1904), of modernist style, which evokes Gaudí. ▶

The **Carlton Hotel** was built as a hotel in 1927, mimicking the style of its namesake in London. During the Civil War it served as the headquarters of the Euskadi Government, and the *lehendakari* (Basque leader) José Antonio Aguirre presided over the military parades from its balcony. A tasteful restoration has successfully returned the building to its original splendour and regained for the city the beauty of this outstanding, elegant construction.

A few metres from Plaza Elíptica, on Calle Alameda de Recalde, stands the **Casa Montero,** built in the purest modernist style in 1904. It is a historical monument in the purest Gaudí line. The Ensanche or city extension reached its north-west limit in the so-called **Parque de Bilbao,** which in fact bears the name of an illustrious benefactress of the city, *Doña Casilda de Iturriza,* a splendid statue of whom, the work of Agustín Querol, presides over the *Paseo de Palmeras.* A double lake makes up the centre of the park, in close proximity to a round pergola designed by Pedro Guimón in the twenties. A cybernetic fountain with light and sound gives life to the pergola, which is avenue for open-air cultural activities in summer.

The park has many pleasant walks and lovely corners, and its leafy, varied tree life makes it a miniature botanical garden. It is a very pleasant spot, a haven of peace and quiet at any time of the year, to escape from the hustle and bustle of the city. There are also small works of art scattered about the park in the form of fountains and sculptures.

Hall of the Hotel Carlton, the most emblematic of Bilbao.

Fine Arts Museum. An exhibition hall of Spanish classical paintings.

In the extreme north of the park stands the **Museum of Fine Arts.** In 1945 the Bilbao Museum was set up here in a sober, two-storey, elegant Neoclassical building. Its creation involved a considerable effort by the whole city, supported both by private collectors and institutions, especially the Ayuntamiento de Bilbao and the Diputación Foral. This ongoing effort has turned this museum, despite its youth, into one of the best galleries in Spain, in terms not only of the paintings on show but also its cultural life.

For this reason it could not be left out of the changes that Bilbao has gone through during the last years, and, as needing a new image and bigger surface, it started a reform which finished with its reopening in 2001. The changes affect as much the outside as the inside (with a more clear and bright spatial organization). The permanent collection continues being the cornerstone of the Bilbao Museum, now included in the so called "Collection 01", with samples of the *Painting of the Spanish and Flemish School* from the XII to the XVII centuries, with paintings of Huguet, Metsys, De Vos, Bermejo, Teniers, the Brueghel, etc.

Of the Spanish paintings are represented El Greco, Ribera, Zurbarán, Velázquez, Carreño, Coello, Ribalta, Valdés Leal and Murillo among others. Of Goya there are some very interesting works. The Italian school is represented in less extent. It is logical that the Basque painting is exposed in large extent, with an excellent selection of the great Basque pictorial masters: Regoyos, Echevarría, Iturrino, Arteta, Zuloaga, the Arrúe, the Zubiaurre, Amárica, Ucelay and others.

But the most risked bet is the game that the new exhibition has established between the historical collection and the vanguard works: so the visitor can find an iron sculpture of Julio González surrounded by paintings of Zurbarán, or the painting of San Sebastián of Ribera next to works of Oteiza. Other contemporary artists which are represented are Solana, Váquez Díaz, Blanchard, Tápies, Gargallo, Chillida, etc. Finally the "Gaur, Hemen, Orain" (Today, Here, Now) brings together works of 22 present Basque artists (Ibon Aranberri, Juan Aizpitarte, Gema Intxausti, Luis Moraza, Darío Urzay, Azucena Vieites).

Three aspects of the Bilbao Park or of Doña Casilda and a detail of the monument to Zuloaga.

Ribera street.
Buildings of the old
bourgeois period of
Bilbao.

FROM THE ENSANCHE TO INDAUTXU AND SAN MAMÉS

Between Plaza de Moyua and Plaza del Sagrado Corazón runs the so-called **Prolongación de la Gran Vía** or "Main Street extension", which contains some of the finest architectural manifestations of the modern city: highly interesting examples of middle class buildings from early this century. Thus, **Casas de Sota** (at number 45), **Casas de Manuel Smith** (at number 44) or **Casas de Bastida** are all blocks of middle-class dwellings. The city's urban regeneration of recent years has led to a revaluation of its heritage, thereby discovering anew the elegant, sturdy residential architecture of the first decades of the C20th.

A second Bilbao expansion took place in the streets adjacent to Gran Vía but in the opposite direction to the first expansion or classical *Ensanche*. It starts at Plaza de Moyua but takes in practically the whole area from the **Church of la Residencia** to **San Mamés,** including the commodious district of **Barrio de Indautxu.** It is in this second city expansion that the Boulevards appear, such as the **Alameda de Recalde** or the **Alameda de Urquijo,** as well as the small peaceful squares like **Egileor** or **Arriquibar** and contemporary architecture which, although serving diverse purposes, is of undoubted artistic value. Architects brought their creativity to bear on housing blocks and singular buildings, some of which must necessarily be mentioned:

The **Church of Sagrado Corazón de Jesús,** known in Bilbao as *La Residencia* and set right in the heart of the city, is the official residence of the Society of Jesus. Its shape is unmistakable, with an elegant, English-influenced Neogothic style that combines white stone with red brick. The interior is decorated in Neo-byzantine style.

The **Teatro de los Campos Elíseos** has the most original facade in the whole city, an outlandish, circular modernist affair with a fretwork frieze, called by many *La Bombonera* (Sweet box). Hard by the theatre stands the **Central Post Office,** a magnificent 1927 construction by Secundino Zuazo.

The old Alhóndiga Municipal, a wine warehouse which the City Hall of Bilbao inaugurated in 1909 according to drawings by Ricardo Bastida, occupies the whole block. Done of red bricks with four corners with spires and a facade with a very curious decoration, it is closed for public because presently a cultural and sports center is being built there.

Gran Vía ends at the **Plaza del Sagrado Corazón,** which takes its name of *Sacred Heart* from a statue standing in the centre. The latter was erected by public subscription in 1926 and comprises a huge stone column topped by a great bronze statue of the Sacred Heart, the work of Ángel Calahorra.

Mazarredo Avenue. Architectural group of bourgeois houses in French style, characteristic of the urban extension area of Bilbao at the end of the XIX century.

Champs Elysées theater. Detail of the modernist facade.

View of Bilbao and its ria from the Caramelo mountain.

Main facade of the International Fair of Bilbao.

Alongside the Plaza del Sagrado Corazón, preceded by a small, peaceful park, stands the **Santa Casa de Misericordia,** an illustrious charity institution that once served as the San Mamés home or refuge. It was opened in 1872 in the presence of King Amadeo I de Savoy. We are now in the Vega de San Mamés, which gives its name to the football stadium. Known amongst the fans as **La Catedral,** it is the home ground of Athletic de Bilbao, a historic team that has won important trophies both in Spain and Europe. Its famous arched grandstand is the focal point of the whole area.

The **Bilbao International Trade Fair** site is only a few metres from the stadium. It consists of 8 pavilions plus a glass office building. It hosts important trade fairs and exhibitions, both national and international, mainly in the industrial and commercial sectors. The Bilbao Trade Fair acquired its international status in 1966, thereafter beginning a stage of ongoing expansion that gave rise to today's buildings, constructed in the early eighties. It is run by a Board that depends on the City Council, the Chamber of Commerce and the Regional Government. In terms of events and business turnover it is the third-most important trade fair site in Spain, and its year-round activity serves as the basis for Bilbao's business tourism. It has an important Congress and Meeting Centre.

The best and biggest fairs are usually biennial, such as the Biehm / Ferroforma or the Trasmet / Siderometalúrgica, the star turns of Bilbao's fairs.

Very close to the trade fair site, in the district of Basurto, stands **Bilbao Hospital,** which Enrique de Epalza began building in 1899 and which was finally opened by King Alfonso XIII in 1908. It comprises several blocks laid out among gardens, following the English style of the time. Built in brick and white stone with tiled borders, it has recently been restored and modernised.

Basurto Hospital, work by Enrique Epalza.

THE RIA, AXIS AND RAISON D'ÊTRE OF BILBAO

The ria or estuary of the river Nervion is the basis and the very raison d'être of Bilbao. The river route that long ago allowed navigation right into the centre of the original city has seen many changes throughout the course of history. That small, humble port next to the church of San Antón has been transformed into the most important conurbation of the whole Cantabrian coast. The seven centuries since its foundation have radically revised the work of nature.

The Consulado de Bilbao was set up in 1511 and was permanently involved in ensuring the river's navigability, which it did by constructing wharves on the banks and straightening its natural winding course. This put paid gradually to the natural beaches, sandbanks, isles and finally the estuary itself. In the late C19th and early C20th century the Bilbao ria underwent its greatest modifications under the direction of the engineer Evaristo de Churruca.

A classical small boat called 'gasolino' crossing the ria of Bilbao.

Next to the harbour and on both banks, the first urban areas kept growing. The harbour area was concentrated in the piers of **Achuri, El Arenal** and the disappeared **isle of Uribitarte.** The shipyards were placed in **Deusto** and **Olaveaga,** and the *Blast Furnaces* were built between Baracaldo and Sestao, in grounds drained from the old estuary. Today, as we stand on the threshold of a new millennium, the ria has undergone a complete facelift and, whilst remaining the city's raison d'être, it will undoubtedly become the true heart of life in 21st century Bilbao.

As a result of the Bilbao Municipal Area Revitalisation Plan implemented between 1989 and 1992 by the Diputación Foral or Provincial Council of Biscay and the Regional Government of the Basque Country, the city has taken on the shape with which it will enter the new century. Redevelopment has affected the entire area of Bilbao but above all the left bank of the River Nervión, the most emblematic projects of the new metropolis having replaced the obsolete industrial structures of the past.

The people of Bilbao call their city affectionately: *el bocho,* word in Basque (euskera) which means a 'hole'; because Bilbao is surrounded of mountains and it is placed in a valley which the river Nervión draws with its meanders. From bank to bank Bilbao is a city of bridges. From San Antón to Abra, along

Hanging bridge above the Bilbao ria.

the ria there are twelve, being the one nearest to the sea the **Hanging bridge,** which crosses between Getxo and Portugalete. It is of iron and elegant, like a triumphal arch that closes the ria.
Recently three new bridges mark with their silhouette above the ria, being two of them footbridges that join both banks, now converted in wide walks along the shore.
Puente de Euskalduna, situated next to the Congress Centre, caters for three forms of transport: apart from being a vital link in the ring road skirting the city, it features a pedestrian walkway complete with two bicycle lanes. The bridge's bluish silhouette has totally transformed the riverside scenery at Deusto.
The **Deusto bridge,** which used to be a lifting bridge, meant in 1937 the connection of the center of the city with the new urban areas of the right bank in Deusto and San Ignacio. Next to it, the **footbridge of Pedro Arrupe** shows its polished style and its structure totally made of stainless steel and wood. Designed by Fernández Ordóñez, it joins the university of Deusto with the future bank park of Abandoibarra.

*The Euskalduna
Bridge joins the bank
of Deusto with the
Doña Casilda Park by
the Congress Palace.*

Universidad de Deusto.

Waters above, the **footbridge of Zubizuri,** (the white bridge of Uribitarte), designed by Santiago Calatrava, reflects in the river's waters its graceful form of inclined arch which reminds a bridge of a boat. Its structure of iron and crystal joins the Campo de Volantín with the future stairs of Isozaki Atea. As we continue our walk along the right-hand banh, beneath the Puente de Deusto, opossite Abandoibarra, we come to one of the classic Bilbao institutions, the internationally known **University of Deusto.**

The University Campus has different buildings corresponding to the various academic fields. The Business University building, the work of José María Basterra and Emiliano de Amann, is a classical 1916 construction with inside patios. The great central block corresponds to the Literary University; it has three projecting facades with sober but elegant lines, topped off by pediments in fin-de-siècle Neoromanesque style. The last building, with a glass structure and iron arcades, is more recent; it was opened in 1990.

A wide flight of steps leads in to the interior, which is laid out around two great cloisters, one housing the Main Hall and the other the Auditorium. A wide, interior, crosswise stairway takes you up to the chapels on the upper floor, one built in Neogothic and the other, smaller one in Neoromanesque style. The library has three floors with balustrades and fresco decorations.

Since fifty years ago Bilbao saw disappear its traditional trams. Nowadays, since Christmas of 2002, the **Euskotran** appears by the ria and the bridges of Bilbao. This light and glazed tram is green and ecological, while it slides on a grass carpet in various stretches, it is decorated with murals of artists from Bilbao and it is an original way to know and see the new Bilbao of Abandoibarra and the bridges from Euskalduna to Atxuri.

To the left, the Euskotran.

Below, the City Hall: stairs and detail of a sculpture of the facade.

The funicular that climbs to the Artxanda mountain, from where you can contemplate whole Bilbao. In the background, the Garden City.

The **Campo de Volantín** is an elegant and romantic walk which begins under the Puente de la Salve. It is still overlooked by buildings recalling its bourgeois past, such as the fine, English-style mansion in the Plazuela de La Salve that serves as the headquarters of the Autonomous Port of Bilbao, an institution which sees to the upkeep of the ria and its wharves.

Lying at the end of Campo Volantín is the Bilbao City Hall or Ayuntamiento. This noble building was raised over the ruins of the old convent of San Agustín, under the direction and plans of the municipal architect Joaquín Rucoba. It was inaugurated on 12th April 1892. Its structure displays an inspired eclecticism, in which classical lines alternate with a certain Baroque brio at the sides. The central part has a series of 3 smooth horseshoe arches as an external reflection of the interior Arab Room or Reception, today also the Wedding Room. The building is crowned with a graceful spire and clock. An elegant flight of stairs leads into the interior, where a sumptuous staircase takes you up from the hall to the second floor.

Arxanda is a leisure and recreational area for Bilbao. Woods, walks and snack bars offer repose all year round but especially in summer. The park's vantage point, at an altitude of 250 metres, is a privileged lookout over the city and surrounding hills. To contemplate the city from up top is just as interesting as to wander through its paths and squares.

The most original way of climbing Artxanda is to take the funicular that takes visitors up to the top of the mountain from the ria, giving panoramic views of the city on the way up.

Above, the "Zubi Zuri" bridge of Santiago Calatrava which joins the Uribitarte Pier with the Campo de Volantín avenue.

Below, park and bank avenue of Deusto.

Next page, Deusto bridge.

ABANDOIBARRA AND 21ST CENTURY BILBAO

The area called Abandoibarra, which throughout the 20th century has reflected the vital role played in Bilbao by industry, the port and the docklands, is now poised to become the very image of the revitalised, thriving city that will emerge in the 21st century.

Measuring some 346,000 square metres and situated right at the very heart of Bilbao, Abandoibarra has witnessed the birth of what will be the city's new Business District. Indeed, it is this area that houses the recently inaugurated Guggenheim Museum and the Euskalduna Congress Centre, which, having been erected subsequent to the demolition of buildings belonging to the Port of Bilbao, rise up at either end of Abandoibarra like giant ships that have run aground.

The **Euskalduna Congress Centre and Music Auditorium** has been built on land once belonging to the great shipyard of the same name. This may explain why its form immediately brings to mind that of the large vessels that in days gone by would loom up as if stranded on the ramps of the former shipyard. Constructed downstream from the Guggenheim Museum using the latest in naval technology, this building boasts a surface area of over 50,000 square metres and is the work of Federico Soriano and

"Euskalduna" Palace of Congresses and Music.
View of the main Auditorium.

Above, view of Bilbao with the Guggenheim; below, the Guggenheim Museum reflected above the river Nervión.

Dolores Palacios, winners of the international competition held to determine which architects should be entrusted with the project.

The **Guggenheim Museum** has become the veritable flagship of the city of Bilbao. It was designed in 1991 by Frank O. Gerhy, who personally chose the location for the new museum. Literally embracing the Puente de la Salve, the museum building would likewise appear to be a stranded vessel, in this case one that has run aground beneath the said bridge. Its inner metal structure has been covered for the most part with two materials, namely stone and glass, to which Gerhy has added a third, titanium, which has played a decisive role in endowing the ensemble with its very own character and personality. Titanium allows one, at all times of day, to appreciate the different hues that are projected onto it by the light. The museum exterior resembles a metal flower whose interconnected forms are lined with concrete and joined by a curved, twisting roof crafted from titanium. As a result the building takes on the appearance of a monumental urban sculpture whose image is mirrored in the waters of the Nervión.

Visitors to Bilbao are welcomed by a figure that has become part of the city landscape, namely **Puppy,** the enchanting flower dog designed by Jeff Koons.

Inside of the Guggenheim Museum. ▶

*Below, the mascot "Puppy" guards
at the outside of the museum.*

BILBAO, CAPITAL OF LEISURE

Like all cities of the world Bilbao has its own particular stamp. The authentic inhabitant of Bilbao or Bilbaino is above all a person of consequence, and the latter characteristic is to be understood as a basic rule of conduct. To be of some consequence means to have your head screwed on, to be blessed with common sense, to have a practical outlook, to be well balanced, honourable, etc. The Bilbaino is endowed with consequence by virtue of belonging heart and soul to Bilbao. In few other places is this last phrase heard with greater conviction than here. The Bilbaino toys with the turns of phrase of his local dialect and particular accent. And he dresses in typical Bilbao fashion, in Bilbao blue, his clothes being elegant, never loud, with a classic cut and a certain English dash. Indeed, fashion in Bilbao is a very local affair, because here people dress like nowhere else. Lastly, the Bilbaino has the proverbial fame of

Bilbao in feasts.

Enthusiasts encouraging Athletic de Bilbao in San Mamés stadium.

being somewhat brash, a reputation he even preens himself on and accepts with good grace. It all boils down to a particular way of coming across.

Basque gastronomy is deemed to be one of the most imaginative and alluring of all, and the contribution of Biscay cooking to this fame is by no means negligible. Bilbao is therefore a centre of excellent cooking with dishes born both of family tradition and the imagination of the fine chefs that honour the city.

Biscay boasts some of the best restaurants in the Basque Country, with a heavy concentration of them in Bilbao. Their names figure in the good-food guides: Bermeo, Goizeko Kabi, Gorrotxa, Guria, Jolas Toki or El Zortziko, to name only some of the most famous. A Bilbao menu may offer as first course *pisto a la bilbaína* (stewed summer vegetables, Bilbao style), with beaten egg added to the vegetables (onion, pepper and courgettes). Then cod, either *a la vizcaína* with red pepper sauce, or *al pil pil* with oil and garlic, or *al club ranero* with both *pil pil* and pisto. Dessert might be the delicious *canutillos* (cream pastries), the *mamia* or junket or a *pantxineta*. All washed down with a local wine, the *txakolí,* or a red *Rioja* from Álava.

Rotisseries and cider houses form the alternative to haute cuisine, offering traditional cooking with fewer specialities but no less quality, an excellent example of popular Basque cooking. They abound on the outskirts of Bilbao with a rustic architectural style and are often housed in restored farmhouses.

The pickled gherkins, *tapas* and *cazuelitas* (hot snacks in earthenware dishes) are an authentic delight to the eye and the palette. Almost all Bilbao bars offer different specialities that are accompanied with good wines. The streets to sample bar snacks are, by way of a guideline, Licenciado Poza in Indautxu; Ledesma in the Ensanche and Somera or El Perro in the Old City.

Bilbao is the cultural capital of the Autonomous Community of the Basque Country and has an endless schedule of activities in the form of numerous exhibitions and yearly festivals. These include the *Festival Internacional de Cine Documental y Cortometraje* (International Festival of Documentary and Short Films) and the *Internacional de Títeres y Marionetas* (International Puppet Show) in December.

Above, a 'tapas' bar in the Nueva Square.

To the left, feasts in the Arenal.

An "otxote", eight throats, singing the typical "bilbainadas".

Young musicians in the streets of Bilbao.

The Bilbao **Semana Santa** (Holy Week) is a long-standing tradition dating back to the Middle Ages. The oldest brotherhood, the *Vera Cruz,* came into being in the C15th. Each day of Semana Santa, from *Viernes de Dolores* (Friday of Sorrows) to Good Friday, a procession of numerous brotherhoods passes through several of the city streets, displaying a rich diversity of statues and religious images, mainly from the C18th to C20th. Especially moving is the *Procesión del Nazareno* (procession of the Penitent) that parades through the district of San Fransisco and the Calle de Las Cortes on Easter Monday.

The Gargantúa (an emotional character of the feasts of Bilbao).

During the Great Week (Semana Grande) the fiesta is lived in the streets of Bilbao.

Bilbao's **bullfighting tradition** is widely known and acknowledged. It is considered by aficionados to be one of the most genuine and demanding rings, and by bullfighters to be an essential venue in their careers. Each year Bilbao celebrates a special bullfighting week called *Corridas de la Semana Grande,* where the most famous bull breeders and bullfighters come together. The *Club Cocherito,* which takes its name from a famous Bilbao bullfighter of yesteryear, keeps a jealous watch over the city's bullfighting tradition. In the Vista Alegre Bull Ring there is a **Bullfighting Museum.**

The **Semana Grande or Aste Nagusia** is a weeklong festival in honour of the Virgin in the month of August. It is the third of the three great festivals held in the three Basque capitals. During this week the whole city throbs to popular festivals, musical shows, *verbenas,* concerts, bull-running… The Old City and El Arenal are the nerve centre of the festival. The bullfights of each afternoon are a must for one and all. The parades and street bands are the heart and soul of festivities, with their spectacular disguises and cardboard instruments. The *Semana Grande of Bilbao* is presided over by the beguiling *Marijaia,* a colourful personality whose gigantic likeness is to be seen everywhere throughout the festival.

The Biscay capital is inseparable from the sea and therefore also from its beaches. At about 10 kilometres downstream from the capital stands the familiar silhouette of the Puente Colgante, which serves as a gateway to **El Abra** or the outer port. The **Puente Colgante** or Puente de Bizkaia is perhaps the symbol most often associated with Bilbao, although it is in fact in Portugalete. The work of the engineer Alberto de Palacio, it was raised between 1890 and 1893 to unite both banks of the ria, Portugalete and Las Arenas, without hindering the boats sailing down the Nervion. Its graceful, metallic structure, inspired by the works of Eiffel, has become the veritable symbol of Biscay.

It is at this point that El Abra begins, the sweeping bay with Bilbao's superport on its left-hand shore and the beaches on the right. These begin in **Neguri,** the most exclusive zone of the municipality of Getxo, which displays one of the most successful urban and architectural developments of the early C20[th] in Biscay. Here were designed, with a good dose of imagination and taste, the mansions of the Biscay upper middle class, the families who ran industry, finance and business. They were inspired by the English country house, built in Neogothic or the Neobasque mansion style.

Alongside the **Puerto Deportivo de Getxo** (Getxo Marina), which is in an advanced state of construction, lie the string of beaches where the people of Bilbao soak up the sun and enjoy the Cantabrian sea.

Jai alai: sport of force and agility.